JUST DANCE

Spotlight on Hip-Hop

Hannah Gramson

Lerner Publications ◆ Minneapolis

For Abby and Lucy

Lerner Publications Company
An imprint of Lerner Publishing Group, Inc.
241 First Avenue North
Minneapolis, MN 55401 USA

For reading levels and more information, look up this title at www.lernerbooks.com.

Main body text set in Mikado.
Typeface provided by HVD.

Editor: Annie Zheng **Designer:** Mary Ross
Lerner team: Sue Marquis

Library of Congress Cataloging-in-Publication Data

Names: Gramson, Hannah, author.
Title: Spotlight on hip-hop / Hannah Gramson.
Description: Minneapolis, MN : Lerner Publications, [2025] | Series: Just dance (Lerner sports rookie) | Includes bibliographical references and index. | Audience: Ages 5–8 | Audience: Grades K–1 | Summary: "From city streets to the dance stage, hip-hop is one of the world's most popular dance styles. Readers will learn fun facts and dance tips on their road to getting started in hip-hop"– Provided by publisher.
Identifiers: LCCN 2023038337 (print) | LCCN 2023038338 (ebook) | ISBN 9798765625668 (library binding) | ISBN 9798765628850 (paperback) | ISBN 9798765634080 (epub)
Subjects: LCSH: Hip-hop dance—Juvenile literature. | Hip-hop—Juvenile literature. | Rap (Music)—Juvenile literature.
Classification: LCC GV1796.H57 G73 2025 (print) | LCC GV1796.H57 (ebook) | DDC 793.3—dc23/eng/20230920

LC record available at https://lccn.loc.gov/2023038337
LC ebook record available at https://lccn.loc.gov/2023038338

Manufactured in the United States of America
1-1010139-51900-1/11/2024

Table of Contents

Chapter 1

Breaking Out into Hip-Hop

On a city street, a dancer does a backflip. Another dancer spins around on her head! The crowd cheers.

It's a hip-hop dance battle.
Who will win?

Hip-hop started in New York City. The dance style is popular around the world.

Lots of pop stars and rappers dance hip-hop when they perform.

Hip-hop has many styles. Some of these are freestyle and breakdancing.

★ Fun Fact ★

People who breakdance are called b-girls, b-boys, or breakers.

Chapter 2

Get Ready to Move

Hip-hop dancers wear tennis shoes.

They wear loose or stretchy clothes that are easy to move in.

Hip-hop requires a lot of movement. It's usually fast-paced. It takes a lot of energy.

★ Tip ★

It's important to stretch before you dance!

Chapter 3

Express Yourself!

Hip-hop music often has a heavy beat. Dancers learn how to move with the beat. Once you know how to stay on beat, you can be creative.

You can make up your own dance moves as you go. This is called freestyle.

★ Up Close! ★

How to Do the Step Touch

- Start with both feet together.
- Move your left foot to the left.
- Bring your right foot over.
- Move your right foot to the right.
- Bring your left foot over.

Chapter 4

Dancing in the Street

Some people do hip-hop just for fun. Others compete. Dancers can compete against one another in dance battles.

Some dance battles happen on a stage in front of judges. Others happen on a city street.

Fun Fact

People can compete alone or with a crew!

You can learn tons of moves. Or you can make up your own. So get creative and have fun!

Glossary

beat: the tempo or pulse in music

breakdance: a form of street dance that can include fast foot movements, spinning on the head or back, and balancing on the head or hands

stage: a raised platform or area where people perform in front of an audience

Learn More

Hammond, Mel. *Spotlight on Stepping*. Minneapolis: Lerner Publications, 2025.
Ken, Pen. *Queen Latifah: An A-B-C Biography*. New York: HarperFestival, 2023.
Lanier, Wendy Hinote. *Hip-Hop Dance*. New York: AV2, 2021.

Index

Photo Acknowledgments

Image credits: Edwin Remsberg/Alamy, p. 5; Evan Agostini/Invision/AP Images, p. 7; LanaStock/Getty Images, p. 9; gradyreese/Getty Images, p. 11; Ariel Skelley/Getty Images, p. 13; PeopleImages/Getty Images, p. 15; Anicka S/Shutterstock, p. 17; Ian Davidson/Alamy Live News, p. 19; Imaginechina Limited/Alamy, p. 21; mikimad/Getty Images, p. 23. Design elements: Kilroy79/Getty Images; Iuliia Mashinets/Getty Images. Cover: Anton Vierietin/Shutterstock.